The Offic[ial]
England Rugby
Annual 2018

England
Rugby

Written by Michael Rowe
Designed by Chris Dalrymple

A Grange Publication

©2017. Published by Grange Communications Ltd., Edinburgh, under licence from the Rugby Football Union. The RFU Rose, the words 'England Rugby' and Ruckley name/image are official registered trade marks of the Rugby Football Union.

Good for Rugby. Proceeds from this book help to fund rugby at every level, from the 8 year olds aspiring to play for England 2027, to the coaches working in our communities. Englandrugby.com/GoodForRugby. Printed in the EU.

ISBN 978-1-911287-85-8

CONTENTS

ENGLAND FIXTURES 2017/18

Old Mutual Wealth Series, Twickenham Stadium

England v Argentina	Saturday 11th November 2017, 15.00
England v Australia	Saturday 18th November 2017, 15.00
England v Samoa	Saturday 25th November 2017, 15.00

Six Nations Championship

Italy v England	Sunday 4th February 2018, Stadio Olimpico,15.00*
England v Wales	Saturday 10th February 2018, Twickenham, 16:45
Scotland v England	Saturday 24th February 2018, BT Murrayfield, 16:45
France v England	Saturday 10th March 2018, Stade de France, 16.45*
England v Ireland	Saturday 17th March 2018, Twickenham, 14:45

*Local time

INTRODUCTION

Welcome to the Official England Rugby Annual 2018.

What a great year for the England team!

2017 saw the records tumble as Eddie Jones' men finished top of the RBS 6 Nations championship and completed a run of 18 victories in a row. A successful tour to Argentina saw the Pumas beaten twice and many England players also starred for the British and Irish Lions in New Zealand.

The Annual reviews this fantastic season, gives you the inside line on your favourite players and is packed full of interesting facts and stats. You'll also be able to catch up with England's Grand Slam-winning women's squad and relive the dramatic HSBC World Sevens Series.

The Annual is also packed full of great pictures, quizzes, player profiles and puzzles. How good is your knowledge of rugby's laws? Find out with our great 'You're the Ref' feature.

2019 is only one year away and everyone's thoughts are beginning to turn to the Rugby World Cup in Japan. With a great blend of young stars and established, world-class players England will be a force to be reckoned with.

Come on England!

RBS 6 NATIONS REVIEW

Round 1 – Twickenham Stadium, 4th February
England 19 France 16
Time for Te'o!

A late try from replacement Ben Te'o helped England squeeze past a determined French side.

France dominated the first 40 minutes in terms of possession and territory. England may not have been firing on all cylinders but two penalties from Owen Farrell and a long range special from Elliot Daly meant the scores were level at 9-9 reaching the break.

England were able to exert more pressure on the French line in the second half. Only a brilliant French tackle could deny Daly a wonderful try in the corner as England's replacements, including James Haskell, began to have a strong impact on the game.

A try from Slimani in the 59th minute, however, meant that France were in the lead with 10 minutes to go. At this point Te'o made his decisive intervention – confidently finishing off a move which had featured Danny Care and James Haskell. Farrell added the conversion and England were relieved to win a close match by 19 points to 16.

Elsewhere in the first round Scotland provided a surprise by beating Ireland and Wales comfortably defeated Italy in Rome.

England's victory was their 15th in a row, their longest-ever winning streak and just the beginning of a truly record breaking year!

Round 2 – Principality Stadium, 11th February
Wales 16 England 21
Another late victory...

A classic match saw England continue their recent run of RBS 6 Nations success against the Welsh, with Elliot Daly scoring a late try to clinch the match.

England scored the first try after no fewer than 26 phases of play, Ben Youngs diving over the line with the Welsh defence stretched beyond its limit. The rest of the half was a thunderous affair, with every scrap of possession fought over and neither side afraid to throw the ball wide given the chance.

Eddie Jones once again used all his eight substitutes in the second half. James Haskell, Jamie George and Ben Te'o were all prominent for England but it was Daly who was put into space by George Ford and Owen Farrell with five minutes to go. The Wasps centre, playing here on the wing, still had plenty to do but he managed it – rounding Alex Cuthbert to score in the corner. Farrell added the conversion and England were able to hold off Wales until the final whistle.

Elsewhere Ireland thumped Italy and France saw off a rapidly improving Scotland side, leaving England top of the table after two rounds.

Round 3 – Twickenham Stadium, 26th February
England 36 Italy 15
'I just don't think it's rugby' – Eddie Jones

Italy's controversial tactics frustrated England in the first half, but Eddie Jones' men ran in five second half tries to emphasise the difference between the two sides.

Italy's novel approach saw them refuse to commit men at the breakdown, meaning no ruck was formed and allowing their players to frustrate England from what would otherwise have been offside positions. The tactics appeared to confuse the England team. Dylan Hartley and James Haskell memorably sought clarification from Romain Poite, the French official - who advised them to ask their coach for help, not the referee!

The second half saw England come up with a decisive answer to Italy's shenanigans at the ruck. Players in white, with Haskell especially prominent among them, simply crashed through the middle and made progress upfield.

Danny Care was the first to cross the line, only two minutes after the break, and he was followed by Elliot Daly, Jack Nowell (twice) and Ben Te'o.

Elsewhere there were victories for Scotland, over Wales, and Ireland, against France. England's win meant they were comfortably top of the table. They also became the first country in RBS 6 Nations history to win 11 consecutive games in the competition.

Round 4 – Twickenham Stadium, 11th March
England 61 Scotland 21
Calcutta Cup Class

England simply outclassed Scotland, with a hat trick from Jonathan Joseph helping them to the highest score in Calcutta Cup history.

Scotland had sent their best side in years to Twickenham, hoping to clinch the Triple Crown, having already beaten Ireland and Wales. England, however, put in a truly superb performance, significantly improving from the previous rounds where they had been resilient rather than scintillating.

Joseph seemed to be able to puncture the Scottish defence at will, running clever lines and using his formidable pace, power and sidestep. As well as his own three tries he set

up Anthony Watson for his score. Danny Care (twice) and Billy Vunipola also crossed the line. Owen Farrell kicked 26 points.

The records continued to tumble. England's win saw them equal the All Blacks' 2015/16 run of 18 consecutive victories. It was also the first time a team had scored more than 60 points in the oldest of all international fixtures. Most importantly it meant that, for the second time in a row, England had clinched the RBS 6 Nations Championship with a week still to go.

Wales beat Ireland and France defeated Italy, meaning that four teams were battling for second place behind England.

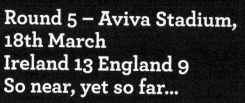

Round 5 – Aviva Stadium, 18th March
Ireland 13 England 9
So near, yet so far...

England just failed to clinch a historic second Grand Slam in the face of a determined Irish performance.

England tasted defeat for the first time under Eddie Jones, and were denied the opportunity to win a world record 19th consecutive victory. Once again it was Ireland who were the party poopers, having also brought the All Blacks' winning streak to an end in an epic match in Chicago in 2016.

Owen Farrell, competing against his father Andy as Ireland's defence coach, scored all of England's points, with one penalty in the first half and two more after the break.

Jones had recalled Billy Vunipola and Anthony Watson to the starting lineup. Ireland often found England's pack difficult to contain, especially in the maul. England were, however, never able to assert themselves as they would have wanted. Ireland were simply too resolute and were able to hold on to the lead they had established in a dominant first half.

The disappointment of the loss, and missing out on a second Grand Slam could not hide England's continued progress under Jones. They were second in World Rugby's ratings, comfortably the best side in Europe and credible challengers for RWC 2019.

England's match had been preceded by a Scottish victory over Italy, and then a narrow win for France over Wales (in a remarkable match which lasted for over 100 minutes). Ireland's win secured them second place in the Championship.

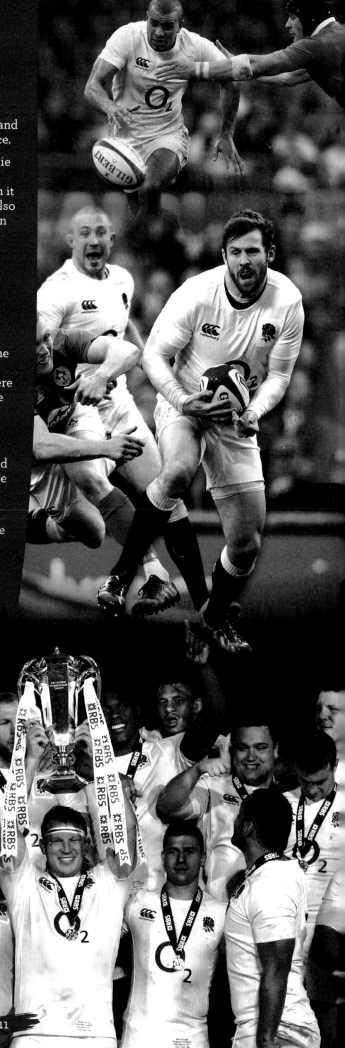

RECORD BREAKING RUGBY!

It's been a brilliant two years for the England team. Here are just a few of the records and stats that the team have racked up. What is your favourite memory from this amazing period?

1 England matched New Zealand's world record of 18 consecutive victories by beating Scotland 61-21 at Twickenham on 11th Match 2017.

2 During the 18 match winning streak England scored a remarkable 72 tries, with a cumulative score of 621-300!

3 England's victory against Scotland was the first time a side had won 11 consecutive victories in the RBS 6 Nations Championship.

CALCUTTA WINNERS

4 England won every game they played in 2016.

5 England's previous record winning streak was 14, achieved by the great Rugby World Cup winning side of 2003. This was surpassed by England's 2017 win over France at Twickenham.

6 England scored 61 points in the 2017 Calcutta Cup. This is the highest-ever score in 146 years of competition!

7 Joe Marler, Owen Farrell, Chris Robshaw, Courtney Lawes and Mike Brown all won their 50th cap during the winning run. Ben Youngs, Dylan Hartley, James Haskell, Dan Cole and Danny Care had already achieved the milestone. You need an experienced squad to win the Rugby World Cup!

8 Owen Farrell became England's second-highest points scorer with a conversion in the 2016 Grand Slam match against France.

9 England scored a try in 26 consecutive matches between 2015 and 2017.

10 In 2016 England became the first team to win the RBS 6 Nations Championship with a round of matches still to play. They did the same again in 2017!

CUP
017

RBS 6 NATIONS

IONS®

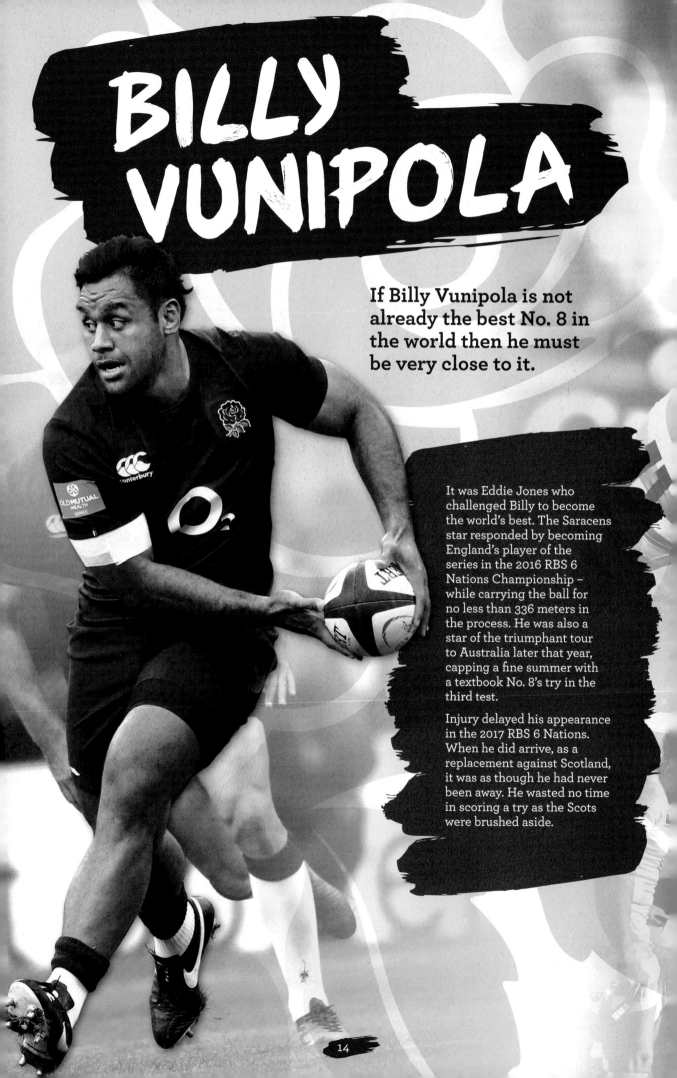

BILLY VUNIPOLA

If Billy Vunipola is not already the best No. 8 in the world then he must be very close to it.

It was Eddie Jones who challenged Billy to become the world's best. The Saracens star responded by becoming England's player of the series in the 2016 RBS 6 Nations Championship – while carrying the ball for no less than 336 meters in the process. He was also a star of the triumphant tour to Australia later that year, capping a fine summer with a textbook No. 8's try in the third test.

Injury delayed his appearance in the 2017 RBS 6 Nations. When he did arrive, as a replacement against Scotland, it was as though he had never been away. He wasted no time in scoring a try as the Scots were brushed aside.

Billy is proud of his Tongan heritage, and comes from an illustrious rugby playing family. His father, Fe'ao played for Tonga in the 1995 and 1999 Rugby World Cups. His grandfather and no fewer than six of his uncles have also represented the Pacific kingdom, while his cousin Taulupe Faletau plays for Wales. Billy's brother Mako, of course, plays alongside him at prop for both England and Saracens.

The brothers share formidable physical prowess and superb ball skills. Billy's handling and distribution abilities are frequently demonstrated, and Mako showed his silky side with a sweet inside pass to set up Jack Nowell at Murrayfield in 2016. If that wasn't enough, both are also accomplished kickers.

Opponents underestimate the Vunipola brothers at their peril!

Billy Vunipola is a force of nature, a truly world-class player.

TEENAGE SUPERSTAR!

Tom Curry made his full England debut against Argentina in June 2017, aged only 18.

Tom and his twin brother Ben were both called up to the England squad for the tour to Argentina. Tom went on to play for England against the Barbarians in May, when he was made man of the match, and to make his record-breaking appearance (England's youngest-ever flanker) in the first match against the Pumas.

SPOT THE BALL

Can you help Ruckley spot which is the real rugby ball in the picture below?

Answers on page 60 and 61.

KNOW THE LAWS!

Rugby is a simple game, and to play it you only need to understand a few basic principles.

The sport does, however, have quite a few laws that can be complicated to understand. Even great players like James Haskell and Dylan Hartley can get confused. Look above and see them asking French referee Romain Poite to explain the ruck law in the game against Italy.

Here we look at a few of the game's key laws, and give you the chance to test your knowledge in the 'You're the Ref' quiz.

OFFSIDE

World Rugby Definition

'In general play a player is offside if the player is in front of a team-mate who is carrying the ball, or in front of a team-mate who last played the ball.'

Offside is perhaps the most important of rugby's laws and the one players need to be constantly aware of. It gives the game its shape and pattern. In rugby the ball can be kicked forward but only passed backwards. If you want a teammate to pass to you, you have to be behind them!

RUCK

World Rugby Definition

'A ruck is a phase of play where one or more players from each team, who are on their feet, in physical contact, close around the ball on the ground. Open play has ended.'

This is the one that caused all the confusion in England's match against Italy...

The ruck is a phase of the game where players contest possession of the ball on the ground. It is formed when at least one player from either side is committed to the ruck. At this point any player in front of the ruck is in an offside position.

Italy refused to commit anybody to the ruck and were able to leave their players in positions which looked offside but were, in fact, not. Very annoying for the England players!

THE TACKLE

World Rugby Definition

'A tackle occurs when the ball carrier is held by one or more opponents and is brought to ground.

A tackled player must immediately pass the ball or release it. That player must also get up or move away from it at once.'

The tackle is one of the most exciting parts of the modern game. Players such as James Haskell and Joe Launchbury will regularly make 20 tackles in a match.

The tackle is also a great opportunity to win possession of the ball. After a tackle the player carrying the ball has to release it immediately. Players such as Maro Itoje are expert at stealing the ball in this situation – especially if the opponent is overpowered or isolated.

THE ADVANTAGE

World Rugby Definition

'Its purpose is to make play more continuous with fewer stoppages for infringements. Players are encouraged to play to the whistle despite infringements by their opponents.'

A very important law, and one which requires the referee to constantly be on top of everything that is happening on the pitch. When an infringement occurs he or she has to decide if it is better for the attacking team to play on. If the attacking team does not subsequently gain an advantage the referee can go back to the original infringement.

Note: the definitions are extracts from the official World Rugby Laws. Check out the full details on http://laws.worldrugby.org

YOU'RE THE REF!

It's not easy being the person in charge of a rugby match, especially if there are more than 80,000 people watching - and criticising! What would you do in the following situations?

The answers are printed upside down at the bottom of the page.

1. You are officiating on a cold and wet day. The home team's full back kicks a penalty which passes between the posts, but is then blown back by a strong gust of wind and lands short of the posts. What is your decision?

2. In a close match, the scrum half of a team leading by just 1 point deliberately delays putting the ball into the scrum. You had clearly told her to put the ball in.

3. Towards the end of the match the hooker pretends to throw the ball to the rear of an attacking line out. As most of the forwards jump for the imagined throw he instead passes the ball five metres to one of his flankers, who catches the ball and crosses the tryline unopposed.

4. A fly half kick-off. His kick travels eight metres before being caught by an opposing prop. The forward puts in an amazing sprint and bursts through several tackles before scoring under the posts. What do you do?

5. Towards the end of a match played in hot summer weather a water carrier comes on to the pitch while play is in progress and gives a bottle to one of the players. You did not give permission. No advantage is gained by either side.

1. You should award the home team 3 points. World Rugby has a special dispensation for windy weather and the kick is deemed to be successful.

2. The laws state that a scrum half has to put the ball in without delay', and must do so when the referee tells them. Award the trailing side a free kick.

3. Players may not pretend to throw the ball into lineouts. No try. Award a free kick to the defending team.

4. Award the try. A kick-off should travel 10 metres but if it does not and an opposing player catches the ball they can play on.
If a member of the fly half's team had caught the ball it would have been an offence. In this situation the opposition would usually choose a scrum on the half-way line, their put-in.

5. Speak to the water carrier and remind them of the laws - medically trained staff are allowed on to the pitch to help players at any time, without permission from the referee. Anybody else needs to wait for the ball to be dead and for permission from the referee.

JACK NOWELL

A proud Cornishman, Jack Nowell is a swashbuckling winger with an impressive strike rate.

Now playing for Exeter in Devon, Nowell comes from a Newlyn seafaring family. He spent his early career playing for the Cornish Pirates, and his distinctive tattoos and hairstyle give him a suitably pirate's appearance – matching his exuberant performances on the pitch.

Nowell was one of the stars of England's 2016 Grand Slam triumph and successful tour to Australia, but struggled with injury at the end of the last season. He knows he faces stiff competition for a place in the starting 15, but he is a supreme competitor and one that Eddie Jones will find hard to ignore.

HSBC SEVENS REVIEW MEN & WOMEN

England finished the 2016/2017 HSBC World Rugby Sevens Series in second place, their best finish for over 10 years.

The Sevens Series is a truly international spectacle. Tournaments take place in 10 cities around the world, with each individual event taking place over two days. Games last only 14 minutes and the action is fast paced throughout.

Sevens players have to be wonderful athletes to contend with the relentless action, with every team member needing to be comfortable in defence as well as in attack.

The HSBC World Rugby Sevens Series provides wonderful entertainment for spectators. Each city puts on a different spectacle for their weekend, and the crowd enjoy the off-field carnival almost as much as the frenetic action on the pitch. This year Twickenham was the host for a family feastival of rugby – with fans being treated to gourmet food from each of the competing nations.

The 2016/17 season was an especially important one for Sevens - following on from its Olympic debut at the Rio games. The Olympic tournament's spectacular success (Great Britain clinched the silver medal behind Fiji) meant millions of new fans were watching for the first time.

Simon Amor's men won two of the year's ten tournaments, in South Africa and Canada, and finished runners-up in two more. England were, however, comfortably beaten into second place overall by South Africa. The dominant Blitzboks won five events and finished second in a further three.

England's women had a less successful season. After a bright start, being semi-finalists in the Dubai tournament, the team finished in eighth place. New Zealand comfortably claimed the series, but they finished runners up in the second leg of the Rugby European Grand Prix Season and qualified for Rugby World Cup Sevens 2018.

2017/18 is a massive year for Rugby Sevens, with the Rugby World Cup Sevens and the Commonwealth Games tournament taking place alongside the HSBC Series. True competitors to a man, England's men will hope to put second place behind them and clinch at least one major title.

SARAH HUNTER

In 2016 Sarah Hunter was officially recognised as the best Women's Rugby player in the world.

The World Rugby prize was a fitting tribute for the No. 8, who has inspired England to great success throughout her 90 cap career and contributed to the development of the women's game. In January 2017 Hunter became one of England's first female group of professional 15-a-side players.

When Hunter began playing, women's rugby was very different to the game we know today. Money was limited and media exposure almost non-existent when compared to today's big name sponsors and world-wide TV coverage.

A highlight of Sarah's career was England's victory in the 2014 Women's Rugby World Cup. Hunter was a dominating force throughout the tournament, with her amazing work rate making her seen by many as England's best player.

Hunter made her debut in 2007, and quickly became a prominent player as England enjoyed a golden era. The team won every Six Nations Championship, with no fewer than five Grand Slams, in her first six seasons.

By the time England next won the championship, in 2017, Hunter was playing as captain. It was another Grand Slam with England beating all their opponents to top the table by nine points.

The matches against France, Italy and Ireland were relatively close but Wales and Scotland were well beaten by Hunter's Red Roses – by 63 and 64 points respectively. Neither Wales nor Scotland scored a point, and England crossed Scotland's line eight times in the first half alone!

English rugby has much to be grateful to Sarah Hunter for. An MBE, awarded in 2015, was suitable recognition for her distinguished service as player and role-model.

WHAT KIND OF RUGBY PLAYER ARE YOU?

Rugby is a game for everyone and rugby players come in all shapes and sizes.

Rugby is also a physical game, and can be technical. While every member of the team needs to be fit and to have good ball-handling skills, each position on the field also has its own requirements and attributes: wingers need to be fast, centres are always powerful and scrum halves need great endurance.

Here's a look at four great players and the attributes they need to be world-class in their position:

Full back - Danielle Waterman

Full backs roam the back of the field, catching high balls in defence and being the extra player in attack. They have the agility to jump, catch and avoid tackle.

Key attributes: AGILITY, SPEED

Scrum Half - Danny Care

Scrum halves cover the most ground, putting in and often receiving from the scrum, making breaks and supplying the fly half. They are the best passers and require the highest levels of endurance.

Key attributes: ENDURANCE, AGILITY

Wing - Jonny May

Wingers operate out wide. They have pace to beat a man and finish off try scoring moves.

Key attributes: SPEED

Prop - Dan Cole

Prop have the strength to carry the front row of the scrum and drive the ball towards the line.

Key attributes: STRENGTH

QUICK QUIZ:

Match the definition from the Oxford English Dictionary to the attribute. Answers on page 60.

SPEED

AGILITY

POWER

STRENGTH

ENDURANCE

Ability to move quickly and easily

The capacity of something to last

Move or travel with great speed or force

The rate at which someone or something moves or operates

The quality or state of being physically strong

JAMES HASKELL

James Haskell is one of rugby's most recognisable figures, playing with a raw energy that few players can match.

The flanker loves playing under Eddie Jones, and has repaid the coach's trust with some of the best rugby of his career. Haskell was the dominant figure in England's 2016 tour to Australia, contributing 18 tackles in the first match – more than twice as many as any other player on the pitch!

GUESS WHO?

Can you guess who the players are in the pictures below?

A

B

C

D

Answers on page 61.

ENGLAND TOUR TO ARGENTINA 2017

Argentina is never an easy place to tour.

By securing a 2-0 series victory over the Pumas, England gained a psychological advantage over their Rugby World Cup 2019 pool opponents.

With many England stars playing for the Lions in New Zealand, Eddie Jones knew the tour would be an opportunity to try new, young players. He gave debuts to 11 players on the tour, including Sam Underhill and 18-year-old Tom Curry - who both performed wonderfully in the back row.

As well as the new boys, England's established stars such as Dylan Hartley, Mike Brown, Joe Launchbury and George Ford all played well. Ford in particular was superb, contributing 38 points (including one try) and being named Man of the Match in the first test.

That first match saw England win a thrilling contest by 38 points to 34, with the lead changing hands six times. Denny Solomona clinched the win with a solo try in the last minute. England won the second match, and the series, with a 35-25 win in Santa Fe. Another thrilling, see-saw match witnessed tries for Charlie Ewels, Piers Francis, Danny Care and Will Collier.

The series victory was testimony to England's strength and depth. Well played England!

Denny Solomona
Argentina 1st Test
Summer Tour

ICBC

COURTNEY
LAWES

DOUBLE PLUS GOOD!

England retained the RBS 6 Nations Championship in 2017, having won it the previous year. This is a rare feat - achieved only 20 times in the tournament's long history. Here we look at the great English sides who have claimed two outright victories in a row.

2016 and 2017

Dylan Hartley's men won the 2016 RBS 6 Nations Championship with one week to go - and then won the Grand Slam by beating France. 2017 saw a great England side equal the world record for consecutive victories, losing only to Ireland.

2000 and 2001

At this time Clive Woodward was building the side which would go on to win the Rugby World Cup in 2003. With Martin Johnson as captain and Jonny Wilkinson kicking the points they won the title in 2000 and 2001 but were denied the Grand Slam on both occasions.

1995 and 1996

1995 saw England win their third Grand Slam under Will Carling. By the time England retained the title the following year, having lost to France, the game had turned professional. Players could now concentrate on the game full time instead of having to combine rugby with a job.

1991 and 1992

1991 saw Will Carling's England win the championship and the Grand Slam. The following season saw another Grand Slam, with Carling's side really cutting loose, scoring a record number of tries and finishing with a points difference of plus 89.

1957 and 1958

1957 saw England win the Grand Slam for the first time since 1928. They won the championship the following year, but missed out on the Grand Slam following draws against Wales and Scotland.

1923 and 1924

Back-to-back Grand Slams saw England clinch consecutive titles. This was a true golden era for English rugby, with the team winning six outright, and two joint, titles in ten championships.

1913 and 1914

1913 saw England record their first-ever Grand Slam. They repeated the feat in 1914, the last championship held before the First World War. 27 England internationals would be killed in the war.

1883 and 1884

England beat all the other sides in the inaugural 1883 tournament, winning the Triple Crown by beating Scotland, Ireland and Wales. They did the same in 1884, retaining the title by two points.

Images supplied by the World Rugby Museum, Twickenham

WHAT A SERIES!

England's stars helped the British and Irish Lions hold the All Blacks to a 1-1 series draw in New Zealand.

Five England players - Anthony Watson, Owen Farrell, Elliot Daly, Mako Vunipola and Jamie George -started every game, while six others played some part in the test series and became a fixture in the side. Owen Farrell stepped up to the mark when his team needed him the most, landing crucial late kicks in both the second and third tests.

England's other Lions confirmed their world-class status. Maro Itoje oozed ability and power after coming on in the first test, becoming a fixture in the side. George's performance gave both his England coach and captain plenty to consider, while Daly was a constant threat to the All Blacks and landed a monster penalty in the third test.

New Zealand are a truly awesome team, and emphasised this with a decisive victory in the first test. The Lions were convincingly beaten, despite scoring the try of the series when Sean O'Brien crossed after a wonderful Liam Williams break.

The second test was a different matter as the Lions upped their game. Sonny Bill Williams was sent off for an illegal challenge on Anthony Watson in the 24th minute, and a truly epic contest was settled in the final minutes with a try from Taulupe Faletau and two kicks from Farrell.

The series was decided on an unforgettable night in Auckland, with Warren Gatland's men giving everything they had to hold on to the All Blacks. The home team scored the game's two tries but Farrell and Daly kept the Lions in the game from the kicking tee, with Farrell's final penalty coming with just three minutes to go. What a match!

To win the World Cup England know they will have to beat the likes of New Zealand. Having played in this series many of England's stars have the confidence of knowing they have the ability to match, and defeat, the All Blacks.

ELLIOT DALY

2017 saw Elliot Daly confirm his place at the core of Eddie Jones' England side.

Daly started all five tests and scored a vital, match-winning try against Wales. He consistently threatened the opposition with his pace and agility and his fine form was rewarded with selection for the Lions tour of New Zealand.

One of Daly's great attributes is his versatility. He plays for his club, Wasps, as outside centre but is also happy on the wing or at full back. He is a great kicker from hand and has a remarkably long (50 metres plus!) range from penalties.

Daly made his England debut as a replacement against Ireland in 2016. His next game - against South Africa - saw him calmly knocking over a penalty from near the half way line. He notched up his first try against Fiji the following week, leaving a string of defenders trailing behind him.

Daly is a multi-talented sportsman, who excelled at cricket while at Whitgift School in Croydon. The explosive power evident in his long range kicking also made him a great fast bowler and a useful batsman.

It was at school that Daly first tasted Twickenham's big match atmosphere - twice winning the national under-18s school cup final. Perhaps inspired by these successes he decided to pursue a career in rugby rather than cricket.

Having been a member of Wasps Academy Daly soon graduated to the senior side. He is now a lynchpin of the Coventry-based club, and has been nominated for both the Aviva Premiership and European Player of the Year awards.

Eddie Jones has a great range of talent to choose from in his back division. Daly's many abilities, however, give him every chance of remaining a key member of the side as they look toward Rugby World Cup 2019 in Japan.

WHERE IN THE WORLD?

18 unbeaten matches in a row! Here's your chance to relive England's record-equalling run. Take our quiz and test your knowledge of rugby stadia around the world.

England 60-3 Uruguay
Manchester City Stadium, 10 Oct 2015. Rugby World Cup.

Hat-tricks from Nick Easter and Jack Nowell see Stuart Lancaster's men end a disappointing Rugby World Cup on a high.

Scotland 9-15 England
BT Murrayfield Stadium, 6 Feb 2016. RBS 6 Nations.

Billy Vunipola is England's standout performer in Eddie Jones' first match in charge.

Italy 9-40 England
Stadio Olimpico, 14 Feb 2016. RBS 6 Nations.

Another hat-trick, this time from Jonathan Joseph, sees Italy comfortably brushed aside.

England 21-10 Ireland
Twickenham Stadium, 27 Feb 2016. RBS 6 Nations.

England struggle to fire in the first half, but Ireland can't live with their power in the second.

England 25-21 Wales
Twickenham Stadium, 12 Mar 2016. RBS 6 Nations.

Owen Farrell scores 20 points as England secure the championship with a round of matches still to go.

France 21-31 England
Stade de France, 19 Mar 2016. RBS 6 Nations.

George Kruis and Maro Itoje provide plenty of power, and Farrell keeps turning the scoreboard with nerveless kicking. England secure a 13th Grand Slam.

England 27-13 Wales
Twickenham Stadium, 29 May 2016. Old Mutual Wealth Cup.

England score five tries as they secure a second consecutive victory over Wales.

Australia 28-39 England
Suncorp Stadium, Brisbane, 11 Jun 2016.

England confirm their arrival as a truly world-class side. James Haskell is immense as three tries and nine successful kicks from Farrell see off the Aussies.

Australia 7-23 England
AAMI Park, Melbourne, 18 Jun 2016.

This time it is the turn of England's defence to shine, resisting immense pressure from the Wallabies.

Australia 40-44 England
Allianz Stadium, Sydney, 25 Jun 2016.

A helter-skelter match sees nine tries, with Jamie George getting the decisive score in the 67th minute.

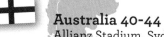

England 37-21 South Africa
Twickenham Stadium, 12 Nov 2016. Old Mutual Wealth Series.

England secure their first victory over the Springboks since 2006. Elliot Daly scores a massive penalty from close to the half way line.

England 58-15 Fiji
Twickenham Stadium, 19 Nov 2016. Old Mutual Wealth Series.

A record win for England over the Pacific Islanders. A total of nine tries, including two from Fijian-born Rokoduguni.

England 27-14 Argentina
Twickenham Stadium, 26 Nov 2016. Old Mutual Wealth Series.

England put in a great collective performance, playing with 14 men for 75 minutes after Elliot Daly's early dismissal.

England 37-21 Australia
Twickenham Stadium, 3 Dec 2016. Old Mutual Wealth Series.

No revenge for the Wallabies for their 3-0 defeat by England earlier in the year.

England 19-16 France
Twickenham Stadium, 4 Feb 2017. RBS 6 Nations.

Ben Te'o comes on as a replacement to clinch the match with an incisive try.

Wales 16-21 England
Principality Stadium, 11 Feb 2017. RBS 6 Nations.

Another thunderous encounter between the two old enemies. England just squeeze home by virtue of an Elliot Daly try.

England 36-15 Italy
Twickenham Stadium, 26 Feb 2017. RBS 6 Nations.

A match that will be remembered for Italy's tactics at the ruck. England soon worked out an answer and won comfortably.

England 61-21 Scotland
Twickenham Stadium, 11 Mar 2017. RBS 6 Nations.

An unexpectedly easy win for England over a strong Scottish side, with Joseph scoring his second hat-trick. England match New Zealand's 18 match unbeaten run.

All the questions below relate to grounds at which England played during their record breaking 18 match winning streak. Can you provide the correct answer?

1) How many times have England played at the Manchester City Stadium?

2) Which RBS 6 Nations ground did England not play at during the winning run?

3) Two of the grounds England won at have hosted the soccer World Cup final. Which ones?

4) Which stadium was originally named after a shape?

5) In which ground did England first play at in 1925?

6) Only one ground saw England play more than once during the winning run. Which one?

7) Which stadium was built on a cemetery?

8) Which stadium had recently been renamed after a building society when England visited in 2017?

Answers on page 61.

OWEN FARRELL

It takes a special kind of person to be a successful international goal kicker, someone with impeccable talent and the ability to perform under pressure.

Owen Farrell is just that kind of person. He has been the foundation on which England's recent triumphs have been built. He appears almost nerveless and is accurate from either side of the posts. England have relied on his kicks to win many close contests, as well as to beat weaker opponents – converting territory and possession into points.

Much more than just a kicking machine, Farrell has starred for England at both fly half and inside centre. He is second only to Jonny Wilkinson in points scored for his country.

ENGLAND RUGBY QUIZ

18 IS THE MAGIC NUMBER!

Between 10th October 2015 and 11th March 2017 England played 18 games and won every single one! This was England's longest-ever winning streak and equalled New Zealand's world record, which they set between 2015 and 2016.

Have a go at this quiz - every question is connected in some way to England's amazing winning run and the number 18. See page 61 for the answers. Good luck!

1) Which team did England NOT play as part of their record 18 match winning streak?

a) Uruguay
b) Fiji
c) Wales

2) How old was Tom Curry when he made his full England debut?

a) 21
b) 16
c) 18

3) How many players have played for England aged only 18?

a) 6
b) 13
c) 36

4) The father of which England star made his Rugby League international debut aged only 18?

a) Owen Farrell
b) George Ford
c) Billy Vunipola

5) England played in the first-ever rugby international in 1871. 10 of their first 18 games were against one country. Which one?

a) Wales
b) New Zealand
c) Scotland

6) Which of England's all-time greats made his debut aged only 18?

a) Will Carling
b) Jonny Wilkinson
c) Martin Johnson

7) Which country denied both England and New Zealand a 19th consecutive victory?

a) Ireland
b) Australia
c) Italy

8) In an important match your rugby team scores 2 tries, 1 conversion, 1 drop goal and 1 penalty. What is your score?

a) 26
b) 18
c) 16

9) Draws are quite rare in rugby, but England have tied a remarkable 18 matches against one country. Which one?

a) Ireland
b) Wales
c) Scotland

10) How many times have England scored 18 tries in one game?

a) 1
b) 2
c) 18

DAN NORTON

Dan Norton is one of the HSBC World Sevens Series' all-time greats.

A fantastic athlete, like all sevens players, Norton became the Series' highest-ever try scorer in April 2017 - with his 245th try! Norton made his sevens debut in 2009 and has been one of England's stars since then. He is a big match player and was selected for this year's HSBC Dream Team.

DID YOU KNOW?

1) Jonathan Joseph scored two hat-tricks (three tries in one match) during England's record breaking 18 match winning streak, against Italy and Scotland.

2) Nick Easter and Jack Nowell both scored hat-tricks in the match against Uruguay in Rugby World Cup 2015. It was the second hat-trick for Nick Easter, who bagged four against Wales in 2007!

3) Elliot Daly and many other England players are talented cricketers. The last man to play international cricket and rugby for England was MJK Smith. Smith played his only rugby international in 1956 and his final cricket test match in 1972.

4) In rugby's early days no points were awarded for a try! Crossing the line only allowed a team a try at kicking a goal.

5) England's biggest-ever win was 134-0 against Romania in 2001.

6) Tom Curry recently made his England debut at the age of 18. England's oldest player was FG Gilbert who was 39 when playing against Ireland in 1923.

7) Dylan Hartley has captained England more than 20 times. The record holder is Will Carling, who led the side on 59 occasions.

8) In 1906 Dr Arnold Alcock played for England by mistake! The selectors had meant to call up Andrew Slocock but sent the letter to the wrong player. Alcock never played again, but Slocock eventually won 8 caps.

9) The first rugby match to be televised was England v Scotland in 1938. The Rugby World Cup 2015 final was watched by 120 million people.

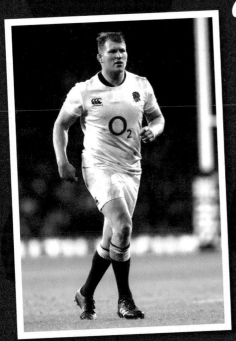

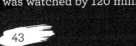

WOMEN'S RUGBY WORLD CUP 2017

The Women's Rugby World Cup took place in Ireland in August 2017.

England went into the WRWC tournament as the holders, having won the 2014 tournament in France. This was England's second victory, having first won in 1994. The victory was especially sweet as the Red Roses had lost the three previous finals to New Zealand.

England met New Zealand again in the 2017 final. On this occasion the Black Ferns were too strong, with a superb second half performance giving them a 41-32 victory and deservedly earning them their fifth title in six tournaments.

The tournament was the climax to a highly successful season for England. They secured a dominant Grand Slam in the 2017 Women's Six Nations, racking up 216 points in total - with Kay Wilson scoring seven tries in one match alone. They went on to win a WRWC warm-up tournament in New Zealand, defeating Australia, Canada and the Black Ferns.

Sarah Hunter's women comfortably won all of their pool matches at the 2017 tournament, scoring 27 tries while beating USA, Spain and Italy. The semi-final against France was a close affair, but England turned in a strong second half performance to win by 20 points to 3.

Ireland 2017 was a great success, with unprecedented numbers of people following the tournament and watching on television. The women's game continues to go from strength to strength!

2017 MATCH STATS

Included here are the key stats from England's successful RBS 6 Nations and other campaigns.

2017 RBS 6 Nations

England 19-16 France - Twickenham Stadium, 4 Feb 2017

	England	France
Tries	Te'o	Slimani
Cons	Farrell	Lopez
Pens	Farrell 3, Daly	Lopez 3

Wales 16-21 England - Principality Stadium, 11 Feb 2017

	Wales	England
Tries	LB Williams	Youngs, Daly
Cons	Halfpenny	Farrell
Pens	Halfpenny 3	Farrell 3

England 36-15 Italy - Twickenham Stadium, 26 Feb 2017

	England	Italy
Tries	Cole, Care, Daly, Nowell 2, Te'o	Venditti, Campagnaro
Cons	Farrell 3	Allan
Drops		Allan

England 61-21 Scotland - Twickenham Stadium, 11 Mar 2017

	England	Scotland
Tries	Joseph 3, Watson, VML Vunipola, Care 2	Reid, Jones 2
Cons	Farrell 7	Russell 3
Pens	Farrell 4	

46

Ireland 13-9 England - Aviva Stadium, 18 Mar 2017

	Ireland	England
Tries	Henderson	
Cons	Sexton	
Pens	Sexton 2	Farrell 3

Old Mutual Wealth Cup

England 28-14 Barbarians   Twickenham Stadium, 28 May 2017

	England	Barbarians
Tries	Earle, Isiekwe, Care	Ashley-Cooper, Tekori
Cons	Ford 2	Madigan 2
Pens	Ford 3	

Summer Tour to Argentina

Argentina 34-38 England - Estadio de San Juan, San Juan, 10 Jun 2017

	Argentina	England
Tries	Boffelli, De la Fuente, Lavanini, Tuculet	Ford, May, Solomona, Yarde
Cons	Sanchez 4	Ford 3
Pens	Sanchez	Ford 4
Drops	Hernandez	

Argentina 25-35 England - Estadio Estanislao Lopez, Santa Fe, 17 Jun 2017

	Argentina	England
Tries	Boffelli, Matera, Tuculet	Care, Collier, Ewels, Francis
Cons	Sanchez 2	Ford 3
Pens	Sanchez 2	Ford 2
Drops		Ford

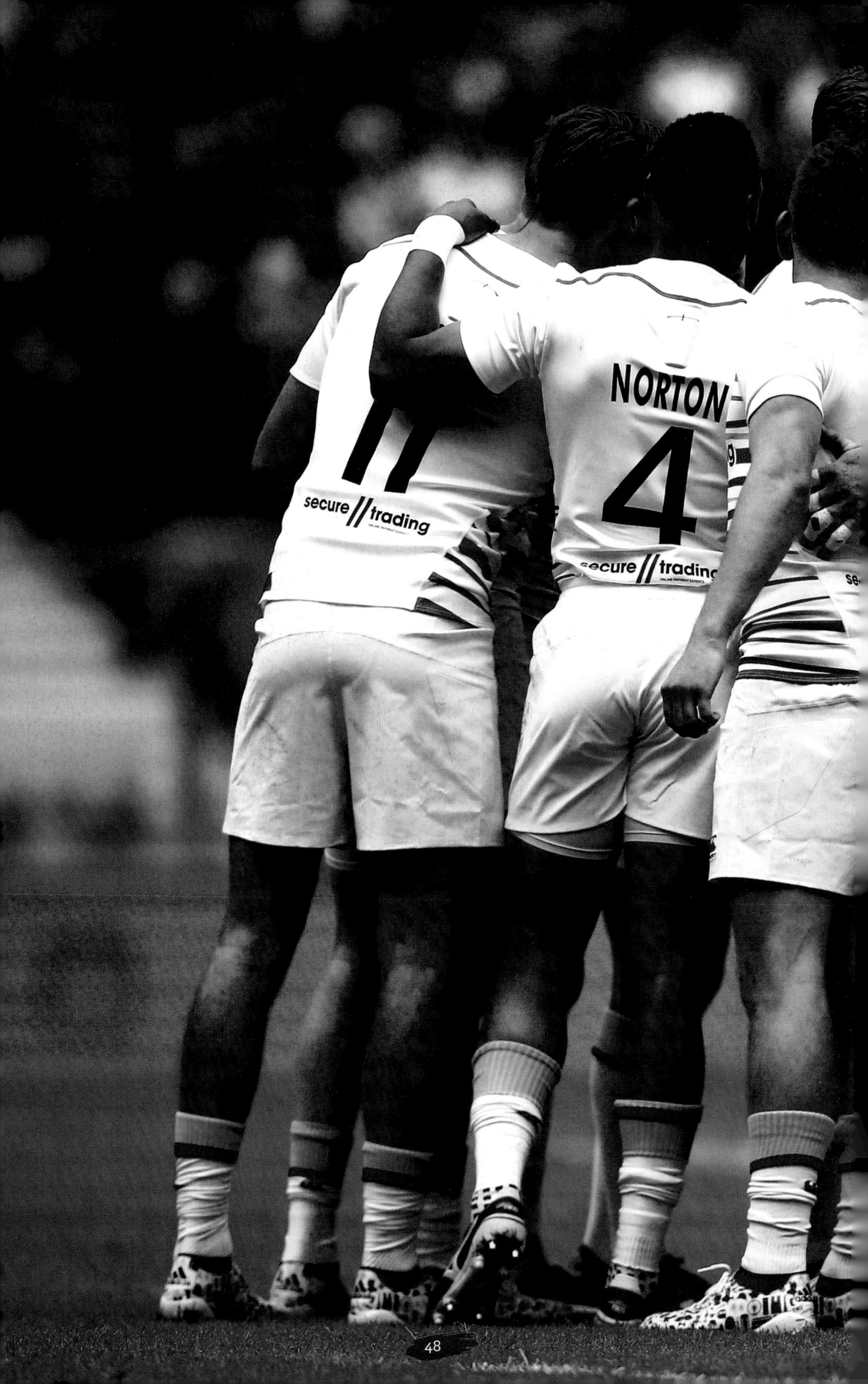
NORTON
4
secure trading
secure trading

Bank of Ireland
Bank of Ireland
Knight
WOMEN'S SIX NAT
WINNE
WOMEN'S
SIX NATIONS

PLAYER SQUAD PROFILES 2018

Name
Mike Brown

Club
Harlequins

Position
Full Back

Height
1.83m

Weight
92kg

Name
Danny Care

Club
Harlequins

Position
Scrum Half

Height
1.77m

Weight
87kg

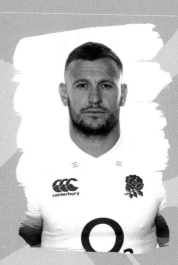

Name
Dan Cole

Club
Leicester Tigers

Position
Prop

Height
1.91m

Weight
118kg

Name
Luke Cowan-Dickie

Club
Exeter Chiefs

Position
Hooker

Height
1.84m

Weight
112kg

Name
Tom Curry

Club
Sale Sharks

Position
Flanker

Height
1.88m

Weight
99kg

Name
Elliot Daly

Club
Wasps

Position
Centre

Height
1.84m

Weight
94kg

Name
Tom Dunn

Club
Bath Rugby

Position
Hooker

Height
1.87m

Weight
106kg

Name
Nathan Earle

Club
Saracens

Position
Winger

Height
1.85m

Weight
99kg

Name
Charlie Ewels

Club
Bath Rugby

Position
Lock

Height
1.99m

Weight
108kg

Name
Owen Farrell

Club
Saracens

Position
Fly Half

Height
1.88m

Weight
92kg

Name
George Ford

Club
Bath Rugby

Position
Fly Half

Height
1.78m

Weight
84kg

Name
Piers Francis

Club
Northampton Saints

Position
Fly Half

Height
1.82

Weight
92kg

Name
Ellis Genge

Club
Leicester Tigers

Position
Prop

Height
1.87m

Weight
113kg

Name
Jamie George

Club
Saracens

Position
Hooker

Height
1.83m

Weight
109kg

Name
Dylan Hartley

Club
Northampton Saints

Position
Hooker

Height
1.85m

Weight
108kg

Name
Nathan Hughes

Club
Wasps

Position
No. 8

Height
1.96m

Weight
115kg

Name
Nick Isiekwe

Club
Saracens

Position
Lock

Height
1.99m

Weight
113kg

Name
Maro Itoje

Club
Saracens

Position
Lock

Height
1.95m

Weight
115kg

Name
Jonathan Joseph

Club
Bath Rugby

Position
Centre

Height
1.84m

Weight
92kg

Name
George Kruis

Club
Saracens

Position
Lock

Height
1.98m

Weight
113kg

Name
Courtney Lawes

Club
Northampton Saints

Position
Lock

Height
2.00m

Weight
111kg

Name
Joe Launchbury

Club
Wasps

Position
Lock

Height
1.96m

Weight
118kg

Name
Alex Lozowski

Club
Saracens

Position
Fly Half

Height
1.84m

Weight
92kg

Name
Harry Mallinder

Club
Northampton Saints

Position
Fly Half

Height
1.95m

Weight
108kg

Name
Joe Marchant

Club
Harlequins

Position
Centre

Height
1.83m

Weight
89kg

Name
Joe Marler

Club
Harlequins

Position
Prop

Height
1.84m

Weight
110kg

Name
Jack Maunder

Club
Exeter Chiefs

Position
Scrum Half

Height
1.78m

Weight
82kg

Name
Jonny May

Club
Leicester Tigers

Position
Winger

Height
1.88m

Weight
90kg

Name
Jack Nowell

Club
Exeter Chiefs

Position
Winger

Height
1.80m

Weight
98kg

Name
Chris Robshaw

Club
Harlequins

Position
Flanker

Height
1.88m

Weight
109kg

Name
Kyle Sinckler

Club
Harlequins

Position
Prop

Height
1.83m

Weight
113kg

Name
Henry Slade

Club
Exeter Chiefs

Position
Fly Half

Height
1.88m

Weight
87kg

Name
Marcus Smith

Club
Harlequins

Position
Fly Half

Height
1.78m

Weight
82kg

Name
Denny Solomona

Club
Sale Sharks

Position
Winger

Height
1.80m

Weight
90kg

Name
Ben Te'o

Club
Worcester Warriors

Position
Centre

Height
1.88m

Weight
104kg

Name
Manu Tuilagi

Club
Leicester Tigers

Position
Centre

Height
1.85m

Weight
110kg

Name
Sam Underhill

Club
Bath Rugby

Position
Flanker

Height
1.86m

Weight
103kg

Name
Mako Vunipola

Club
Saracens

Position
Prop

Height
1.80m

Weight
121kg

Name
Billy Vunipola

Club
Saracens

Position
No. 8

Height
1.88m

Weight
126kg

Name
Anthony Watson

Club
Bath Rugby

Position
Full Back

Height
1.85m

Weight
93kg

Name
Richard Wigglesworth

Club
Saracens

Position
Scrum Half

Height
1.75m

Weight
83kg

Name
Harry Williams

Club
Exeter Chiefs

Position
Prop

Height
1.91m

Weight
132kg

Name
Mark Wilson

Club
Newcastle Falcons

Position
Flanker

Height
1.91m

Weight
112kg

Name
Ben Youngs

Club
Leicester Tigers

Position
Scrum Half

Height
1.78m

Weight
92kg

QUIZ ANSWERS

P.17: Spot the Ball

P.26/27: What Kind Of Rugby Player Are You?

Agility
'Ability to move quickly and easily'

Endurance
'The capacity of something to last'

Power
'Move or travel with great speed or force'

Speed
'The rate at which someone or something moves or operates'

Strength
'The quality or state of being physically strong'

P.29: Guess Who?

 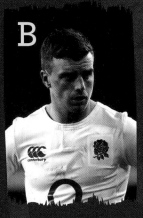  

P.38: Where in the World?

1 - Once. England have played in Manchester before - 7 times at the old Whalley Ranges ground during the 1800s and, more recently, twice at Old Trafford.

2 - Aviva Stadium, Dublin. England's winning run came to an end there in March 2017.

3 - Stade De France, Paris (1998) and Stadio Olimpico, Rome (1990).

4 - The AAMI Stadium in Melbourne was originally called the Melbourne Rectangular Stadium - in Australia stadiums for rugby, soccer and similar sports are often designated as 'rectangular', those for cricket and Aussie Rules are known as 'oval' stadiums.

5 - Murrayfield. England have played at the Edinburgh ground on 45 occasions and won 20 times. Scotland have only ever won four matches at Twickenham.

6 - Twickenham Stadium.

7 - Suncorp Stadium, Brisbane.

8 - The Principality Stadium, until 2015 the Millennium Stadium in Cardiff.

P.41: England Rugby Quiz

1- a

2 - c

3 - b

13 players have played for England whilst aged 18. RH Fowler is England's youngest-ever player. He played his only match (against Ireland) aged 17. His international career was over before his 18th birthday!

4 - a

Andy Farrell made his rugby league debut for Great Britain against New Zealand in 1993. His union debut for England came in 2007.

5 - c

6 - b

Jonny came on as a replacement against Ireland in 1998, playing on the wing! He didn't get the opportunity to kick on that day, but would go on to be England's highest-ever points scorer.

7 - a

8 - b

9 - c

England's first draw with Scotland was in 1873, the last came in 2010. England have drawn a total of 50 matches.

10 - a

England scored 20 tries when beating Rumania 134-0 in 2001. Their next highest total was 17 against Uruguay in RWC 2003.